MONEY AND BEYOND

Also by Arnold M. Patent

You Can Have It All, Revised Edition

Death, Taxes and Other Illusions

MONEY AND BEYOND

Arnold M. Patent

Celebration Publishing

Sylva, North Carolina

Celebration Publishing
Route 3, Box 365AA
Sylva, NC 28779

Cover design by Barbara Patent Anik

Book layout and typesetting by Bukur Design Group

Library of Congress Catalogue Card Number: 93-73898
ISBN 0-9613663-5-4
First Printing
Printed in the United States of America
Printed on recycled paper ✹

To my family,
whose love and support
is a constant joy

ACKNOWLEDGMENTS

There are many people I wish to thank for their contributions to this book:

Kathy Hart, for her masterful job of editing;

Grady Claire Porter, for her valuable suggestions and generous sharing of her meditations;

Participants in the International Network of Mutual Support Groups, for their commitment to open their hearts, feel their power and share their unconditional love.

CONTENTS

PART TWO: GROUNDING THE VISION

FOREWORD

For many years I heard the oft-repeated adage "When the student is ready, the teacher will appear," and I would wonder, "So where is my teacher?"

I met Arnold Patent in the spring of 1990 through a set of audiotapes recorded at a workshop in Arizona in 1986. I listened to the tapes at least a dozen times, I read and reread Arnold's two books, and that summer I attended his annual five-day conference at Asilomar on the Monterey Peninsula in California.

I never dreamed my teacher would be an ex-lawyer with a New York accent who looks like a leprechaun. I did know, however, that his message would have to be simple, heart-felt, down-to-earth practical and absolutely sincere. I also knew that my teacher would have to live and practice his teaching with unwavering commitment.

It has been the greatest honor and lesson to edit *Money and Beyond*. Throughout the months-long process of rewriting and revising, I not only came to deepen my love, respect and appreciation for Arnold Patent, but in testing the material I was editing, I learned to open my heart and allow in a veritable flood of support—some in the form of money, some in the form of gifts, and all in the form of love, the most precious treasure in the Universe.

The ideas in *Money and Beyond* do not require a Ph.D. or a highly trained intellect to comprehend. In fact, too much intellect can get in the way of understanding the simple truths presented on these pages. I suggest you approach the book with an open heart, an open mind and a willingness to look at these ideas through the eyes of love. Then test the ideas for yourself, and be ready for miracles to happen.

Kathy Hart
Editor

INTRODUCTION

I have devoted my whole life to preparing myself to write this book. The first fifty-one years were invested, through deep involvement, in learning our competitive-adversarial system: first as the son of a practicing attorney, and then for twenty-five years as a practicing attorney myself. The last thirteen years have been invested in following what can be fairly called an opposite system—one that honors mutual support and an open heart.

Following this latter approach while carrying the deeply held beliefs and repressed feelings of the former has not been easy. But it has been fulfilling. I not only came to understand the difference between the two systems, I discovered what it takes to make the transition from one to the other.

For the fifty-one years during which I viewed the world through the narrow lens of competition and adversarial relationships, the stress, struggle and pain I endured seemed normal. For the last thirteen years during which I expanded my range of vision to include mutual support and unconditional love, the stress, struggle and pain have steadily diminished to be replaced with calm, ease and fun.

Among the lessons I learned is that there is no limit to mutual support and unconditional love. There is no limit to fun. There is no limit to inspiration, creativity and abundance. And there is no limit to those who can share in this way of experiencing life; in fact, the more who share in it, the more there is to share.

The purpose of this book is not to teach you techniques for amassing millions of dollars. It is to assist you in expanding your consciousness and reconnecting to your own inherent power in a Universe of infinite abundance that keeps expanding.

My approach is to set forth certain basic and underlying principles that govern the Universe and that operate consistently and in the same way in each of our lives. These Universal Principles, as I call them, support each of us equally, and when we align with them, we learn what true abundance is all about. We also learn how powerful we really are.

The first section of the book looks at the broadest of these principles, those that help us to expand our vision about money as well as all other aspects of the material world. The second section sets forth practical ways to apply these principles to our day-to-day lives.

For many of us, coping with shortage is one of our greatest challenges. In time, we come to recognize that shortage is just a result of narrow vision and a closed heart. It is a result of vesting our power in the belief that shortage is a reality. As we allow our vision to expand and our hearts to open, and as we reclaim our power, shortage expands into abundance, and we find that our true challenge is dealing with ever-growing abundance.

My hope is that by the time you finish reading this book, your heart will be open, your vision expanded and that you will have reclaimed enough of your power to realize that *you* are the creator of your abundance.

Arnold M. Patent
Marina del Rey, California
Fall 1993

PART ONE

THE BROADER
PICTURE

1

EXPANDING
OUR VISION

Life often seems frustrating and unsatisfying, especially around issues of money, because we are literally approaching life backwards. If we were to consider building a house, we would not begin the process by selecting the lumber or shopping for sinks. We would begin with the overall vision for our house.

The more comprehensive our vision for the house—including its energy efficiency, the harmony of its design, the house's ease of maintenance as well as affordability—the more gratifying will be the end product. When the vision is broad, the house created will contain all of the values built into that greater vision.

Our approach to life works the same way. For most of us, our view of life, its meaning and purpose, is very narrow. Thus, the results we achieve contain all of the constrictions built into our limited vision.

We are all familiar with the typical views we hold: that life is a struggle to survive; that success is achieved only through hard work and relentless competition; that money and property rights come before human rights; that some people are more valuable than others and thus are worthy of greater rewards.

These views, and many others like them, derive from a core belief that we are each separate from one another. Seeing ourselves as separate leads us to assume that there are people and situations in our lives that are more powerful than we are. We then approach life as a battle we seem destined to lose or as a race that seems too exhausting to win.

How do we move beyond this limited view of life as an endless struggle? The simplest approach is to be willing to expand our vision. Taking the time to allow our vision to broaden is the first and most important step we can take in bringing clarity to this vision. It is also the step most likely to be skipped or rushed through, given our years of indoctrination that time is money and that speed is more important than the direction in which we travel.

When expanding our vision, we best support ourselves by staying focused on this step for as long as it takes to acquire a sense of the breadth and depth of life and our part in it. As we begin to feel the vastness as well as the sense of awe that comes to us when we connect with this vision, we find ourselves experiencing something that goes far beyond our language's capacity to label or describe. We find ourselves connecting with our Oneness, the natural state of our being and the source of our power.

For many years, we have accepted an extremely limited vision of ourselves as essentially weak, powerless, dependent, and subject to innumerable forces and circumstances beyond our control. Let us now look beyond this limited vision and begin, in earnest, to discover who each of us truly is and what life is truly all about.

2

THE VASTNESS OF CONSCIOUSNESS

We experience everything through our consciousness, which includes all of the many ways and means we have to perceive life. Our consciousness extends far beyond our physical senses, far beyond our ability to see, hear, touch, taste and smell. In fact, our consciousness has no inherent limitations. How much of it we employ depends upon how broadly we define it.

In our society, most people equate consciousness with the conscious mind, the intellect. This limited definition leads to what we call the scientific approach—the study of the physical world using methods that are quantifiable and that produce results that are tangible. When we adopt the scientific approach to life and choose to pay attention only to physical factors, the results we obtain must necessarily be limited to the physical.

But there are clearly factors that affect our lives that are neither tangible nor quantifiable, that go beyond the physical. One such factor is imagination, the conjuring of images that have no physical reality and often no logical connection to one another. Imagination, sometimes called a daydream or flight of fancy, is always intensely subjective and personal.

9

At times our imagination leads to very creative expression, such as a piece of artwork, a story, a musical composition or the design of a structure. At other times it leads to discoveries that require the discoverer to expand his perception beyond its prior limits, as in the case of Albert Einstein developing his Theory of Relativity, or Martin Luther King, Jr., redefining black-white relationships in terms of peace and brotherhood.

Closely related to imagination are dreams, another factor that defies our rational understanding. The stories, symbols and messages that arise from dreams add a rich dimension to our daily lives.

Another factor is feelings. Like colors, there is truly an infinite range of feelings and combinations of them. We give them labels, but in fact, no two are identical. As with imagination and dreams, feelings are intensely subjective and go far beyond the ability of anyone to reduce to a scientific study.

Yet another factor that is not quantifiable is inspiration. The sources of inspiration, the products of inspiration, as well as the feelings that accompany inspiration, are so extensive and varied, they are beyond the capability of the most advanced computer technology to catalog.

And then there is intuition, that gut-level feeling that we know something without any logical reason or explanation. Although it cannot be scientifically studied or rationally explained, many people, including scientists, rely on intuition for making important decisions in their lives.

What all of these factors—imagination, dreams, feelings, inspiration and intuition—have in common, in addition to being nonquantifiable and in addition to being very valuable and significant parts of our lives, is that they verify that we are more than mere physical beings. Furthermore, our ability to imagine, to dream, to feel, to be inspired and to intuit is as unlimited as consciousness itself.

THE VASTNESS OF CONSCIOUSNESS

The very vastness of our consciousness makes it difficult to focus on. In our society, we are trained to narrow our focus so that we can more closely examine each individual element or aspect of the whole. We keep avoiding the larger picture, the context in which things occur. We particularly avoid those things that are intensely subjective. Yet the subjective factors are the very ones that give our lives their greatest meaning and significance.

We don't need to fully comprehend the concept of consciousness to appreciate its value. Just our willingness to consider the vastness of ourselves, our unlimitedness, our infinite potential, is sufficient to infuse us with a sense of our magnificence.

3

THE ROLE
OF MONEY

When most of us think about improving the quality of our lives, we think in terms of money, since it is the means we use not only to exchange goods and services, but also to measure our success. Indeed, today in our society it seems that nothing can be done without money. Our health, happiness, security—our very survival—seems to depend solely on how much money we do or do not have.

So money has a pivotal function in our lives. However, its true role goes far beyond the limited one that we have ascribed to it. First of all, since money is essentially a neutral object, having no inherent value of its own, it takes on whatever qualities we invest it with. When we believe that money has the power to keep or make us healthy, to bring us happiness or to allow us to feel secure; when we believe that our survival depends on money, then we know we have, through our beliefs, invested money with the power to run our lives.

Secondly, money provides us with a very accurate picture of how we view life. If we are willing to track our experiences with money, we can quickly discover just how narrow or expansive our vision of life is. When money seems to be in limited supply, we know we are viewing life from a limited perspective. When it moves freely into and out of our lives, we know our vision is more expansive.

These two roles that money plays relate very closely to each other. The belief that money has power flows directly out of a narrow vision of life, a vision that sees us as mere physical beings who are essentially powerless and at the effect of forces over which we have no control.

When we are willing to broaden our vision and to see ourselves as more than physical bodies—to see each and every one of us as a consciousness that has no limitation and immeasurable potential—we begin to feel the power of who we really are. And in our willingness to feel this power, we realize that we are not at the mercy of circumstances beyond our control, but rather that we are the creators of these circumstances.

Moving to this broader perspective is a big step to take, for it pits us against strong beliefs that not only we hold but that those close and dear to us hold as well. In my own experience, it took many years to expand my vision of life, to feel the power within me and to claim it as my own.

In supporting many others in doing the same for themselves, I came to an important understanding: *we access our power through our feelings.* And since the circumstances surrounding money frequently arouse strong feelings, money provides a most valuable vehicle to assist us in reclaiming our power.

As we feel our power grow, we realize that money is not something worth working hard for or worrying about having enough of. Rather, it is simply a tool to help us in expanding our self-empowerment. And as we stay with the process, we come to know, at a deep feeling level, that we are the power in the Universe, the creators of money and everything else.

We have all spent many years devoting ourselves to a way of life that is buttressed by beliefs that run counter to the truth of our inherent power. Moving through the intensity of these limiting beliefs and the loyalties we feel to those who taught them to us calls for a great deal of loving support. It also requires support to move beyond our doubts that we are truly creators with unlimited potential.

This book is meant to offer some of that support by providing the concepts and exercises that will lead us to feeling more and more of our true power. Therefore, many of the chapters focus more on accessing our power, which is the true source of money, than on money itself.

If we choose to expand our vision, we begin by opening our hearts. If we choose to reclaim our power, we also begin by opening our hearts. Our true power point is our heart. Opening it and keeping it open is the most self-supportive and self-empowering choice we can ever make.

4

OPENING
OUR HEARTS

When we open our hearts, we allow ourselves to connect to the gentle, sensitive energies within us. These are the original energies of the Universe. They are the essence of our true makeup as human beings, and all other energy derives from them. It's like the basic harmonic chord in music. Depending on its use, the chord can result in melodious symphonies or dissonance, but neither use changes the basic chord.

Often when we connect with these gentle and sensitive energies, we feel vulnerable. We may cry or feel like crying. While most of us have been trained to believe that feeling our feelings makes us weak, the truth is that making this connection puts us in touch with the true source of power in our lives. It is through our willingness to connect with these gentle and sensitive energies, and to feel them fully, that we access our true power.

Every experience we have, every moment of our lives, is meant to be felt in our hearts. We are feeling beings, and the more we open our hearts and feel our feelings fully, the more we connect to who we really are. The more we open our hearts and feel our feelings fully, the more of our power we reclaim.

In the early stages of this heart-opening process, these gentle and sensitive energies do bring up feelings of vulnerability and weakness. However, that's not because we are weak and vulnerable; it's because we were carefully and repeatedly taught to equate these feelings with weakness.

As we stay with these gentle and sensitive energies and gradually reconnect with the power they hold, we increase our ability to keep our hearts open. In the process, we allow more intense energies, those that we consider the opposite of gentle and sensitive, to rise to the surface. The more intense the energies we feel in our hearts, the more power we access. This is the process of expanding self-empowerment.

There is a simple three-step exercise, called the Feeling Exercise, which, if practiced consistently on a daily basis, can efficiently support us in connecting with these energies and reclaiming the power in them. I suggest you go through the Feeling Exercise right now. (See next page.) Begin to become familiar with it. Let it become part of your life.

There is a whole new world awaiting us when we open our hearts and reclaim our power. This world won't necessarily be any different from the one we now see, but it will feel very different. Our willingness to feel more fully through our open hearts and from a place of empowerment inspires us to remember that we are the creators of our world and its infinite abundance.

THE FEELING EXERCISE

Close your eyes and scan your body. Notice how you are feeling. Then:

1) Feel the feeling free of any thoughts you have about it. Feel the energy, the power, in the feeling.

2) Feel love for the feeling just the way it is. Feel love for the power in the feeling.

3) Feel love for yourself feeling that love and that power.

5

LOVE

All energy in the Universe is the same, and this energy is love. Love is what we are and what we do naturally. It may be flowing freely or it may be blocked, repressed or distorted. However, love is always present everywhere. And it is the source of our power.

Love, being energy, can only be felt. It cannot be defined or described. Whenever we choose to define or describe love, we are substituting an intellectual experience for the feeling experience that love is.

The introduction of the intellect, the conscious mind, impedes the free flow of love. The more intense the intellectual intervention, the more energy we block or distort.

We can look at the conscious mind as a filter through which love flows. As the conscious mind becomes more active, the filter becomes clogged and less love can flow through. When the conscious mind is quiet, the filter remains clear and love flows freely.

Our constant compulsion to intervene with the conscious mind derives from our belief that our intellect is our primary source of support and power. So strong is this belief that we have come up with very inventive and sophisticated ways to keep our focus on our intellects and away from our feelings, which are our access point to love in all its fullness.

The truth is that love is our sole source of support and power. And because it has all of the Infinite Intelligence of the Universe within it, when love flows freely, it moves with the guidance of that Intelligence. Love needs no intervention on our part. In fact, our intervention only serves to distort or block its otherwise perfectly supportive movement.

The introduction of the intellect, which we call thought, leads to beliefs. Beliefs are thoughts that are important to us. We create their importance by adding feeling to the thoughts. The feeling contains the power, which is transferred to the thought. After the transfer, we feel as though we have lost some of our power. I call the combination of thought and feeling *emotion*.

Anger, for example, is a thought that something is wrong backed by a strong feeling. The feeling gives power to the thought and turns a purely intellectual experience into a deeply emotional one.

When we are willing to shift our focus from the thought to the feeling, we make it possible to open the energy that has been locked into the feeling. The energy, remember, is love, which is the source of our power. When we open our hearts and feel love for the feeling, we recognize that there is no difference between the energy flowing out of our hearts and the energy flowing out of our feelings.

We have all been taught how to repress the full and free feeling of love. As we close down our feelings, our main connection with each other and with our environment is weakened. This strengthens our belief that we are alone and separate from one another. The more separation we feel, the more powerless we feel and the more fearful we become of each other. Fear, by definition, is a withholding of love.

It is only by force of will that we can withhold the love within us. The repression of the feeling of love over an extended period leads us to believe that the repression is natural. It is not. In fact, what is natural is for love to continually expand. Thus, it becomes increasingly difficult to hold the love down.

Whenever we attempt to repress or block the free flow of love, we create discomfort in our bodies. If the repression continues, the discomfort intensifies, perhaps taking the form of a headache or backache or more severe pain or illness. However the discomfort manifests, it is a signal to us to quiet our minds, feel our feelings fully and open our hearts to these feelings. The signal of discomfort is always sending us this same message.

Very few of us were taught to interpret discomfort as a signal to feel our feelings. Our overriding belief, born of repeated instructions from our earliest years, is that our feelings are a sign of weakness, that they are untrustworthy, will get us in trouble and are unprofessional. Thus, we have become masters at tolerating great amounts of discomfort.

However, since love is always expanding, the repression takes more and more effort to sustain. Eventually, the love breaks forth, and we find ourselves surrendering to what is totally natural and joyful to us—feeling the fullness of our love and our power.

6

MONEY IS ENERGY

Money is nothing but energy. Since we know that there is no shortage of energy in the Universe, it follows that there is no shortage of money either.

We also know that all energy is love; therefore, money and love are equivalent. When we look at a dollar bill, if we don't see and feel love, we are just closing our eyes and our feelings to what is truly in front of us.

Everything in the material world reflects to us the present state of our consciousness. This is true whether the object is money or a human being. When we look in a mirror, and what we see is someone we feel good about, someone who is lovable, kind, generous, fun and inspiring, we are connecting with the attributes of love freely flowing. When what we see in the mirror is an image that is uncomfortable for us to focus on, a face that appears unattractive, sad, angry, confused or in some way unlovable, we are seeing and feeling an image that is being distorted by a consciousness that is narrow and limited in its focus and vision.

The essential nature of the object—be it a face or a dollar bill—is always love. Its manifest form only appears to hide this essence from the viewer when the viewer isn't seeing and feeling clearly. When the sight and the feeling are clear, love is clearly seen and felt.

Whenever money is seen and felt as love, it supports us by expressing such loving qualities as generosity, harmony, inspiration and compassion. Furthermore, as with love, the more money is shared, the more it expands.

As our love for ourselves grows deeper, our love for everyone and everything around us deepens commensurately. In this deeply loving state, we attract support in all of its many forms, from people to money. And abundance, the natural state of the Universe, becomes our reality.

7

GOD—THE
ONENESS

If we choose to have a successful relationship with money, the place to begin is with our relationship with God. Since all of our relationships derive from this basic one, it is important that we start here and establish the clarity, trust and open-hearted connection with God that is essential to every successful relationship.

What is God? God is the unifying force in the Universe. It is the Oneness, the Wholeness, the energy that is common to everyone and everything.

This unifying force gives life to everything, sustains life and contains the Infinite Intelligence to guide life. Because this energy is so nurturing and unconditional in its support, we often refer to It simply as love.

Very few of us were raised to believe that God is an unconditionally loving and supportive presence in our lives at all times. Instead, most of us were taught to fear God as the ultimate authority figure who stands in judgment of everything we think and do, rewarding good deeds and punishing bad ones.

What is crucial for us to recognize is that how we perceive God determines precisely how we experience our lives. We always project our beliefs onto the world around us. This is another way of saying that we always experience an outplaying of the state of our own consciousness.

If we believe that God is an entity that exists outside of us, an entity that is sometimes loving and at other times angry and vengeful, our lives will mirror this belief by occasionally being filled with love and at other times filled with hardship and suffering. On the other hand, when we feel and know that God is the Oneness and that the Oneness is love, and that each of us *is* this Oneness—at all times and under all circumstances—life becomes a continuously loving, joyful journey.

God, our Oneness, love, is a totally subjective and personal experience that we can only feel. We cannot explain God, nor can we convince another of Its reality. What we can do, however, is allow our definition of God to continually expand into the broadest feeling of love possible. A simple way to do this is to use the Feeling Exercise (see page 23) to open our hearts and to allow our God presence to emerge in all Its fullness.

In truth, we are always connected to our God presence, our Wholeness, and to all the power It comprises. Our only option is whether to be aware of this connection. Whenever we attempt to isolate or separate any person or any thing from this Wholeness, we feel a loss of power.

The attempt to separate anyone or anything from God is an intellectual exercise in futility. We cannot succeed, but we can make believe that we can. The belief that we are separate from our Oneness is reflected in our sense of separation from each other.

This sense of separation leads us to see our physical world as having primary importance, and we vest enormous power in it. We then give precedence to our intellects, because we believe that they are the best means of dealing with our physical world. And we close down our feelings, which connect us to our Oneness, based on the belief that our feelings just impede the efficient use of our intellects.

As we come to realize that we are the God presence, we open our hearts to ourselves and trust the love and power that we feel to guide us. There is unimaginable richness in the infinite variety that makes up our God presence, our Oneness. As our connection with It expands, we bring this richness more fully into every aspect of our lives, including our relationship with money.

It is only when we know and feel that we are the God presence, the creators of the Universe, that we can acknowledge how truly powerful we are. Only then can we appreciate that our ability to create and enjoy money, under all circumstances, is truly unlimited.

8

SECURITY

Many people believe that money represents security. But what is security, really, and where does it come from?

Security is a feeling, and it comes from within us. It is a feeling of self-empowerment. With our focus so constantly on money and the material world around us, we keep overlooking where our true power lies.

One of the most significant ways that we diminish our sense of empowerment is by transferring our power to the physical world, and specifically to our physical bodies. We do this by believing that our bodies are who we really are. From this vantage point, we see ourselves as separate from our Oneness and from each other.

This limited perception leads us to close our hearts and suppress our feelings, which heightens our sense of vulnerability and increases our fear. It is in this vulnerable, fearful state that our two major concerns—death and pain—seem most real to us.

As long as we vest our power in the physical world, and particularly in ourselves as physical beings, we can be certain that our concerns about death and pain will remain strong. On the other hand, we always have the choice to reclaim our power. We start by feeling the feelings that our fear of death and pain evokes, and then bringing the feelings and the power they contain into our hearts. With practice, we move beyond the vulnerability and limitation of our physicality.

Death and pain are nothing more than limited perceptions—misperceptions—that dissolve in the presence of a fully open heart. We cannot talk ourselves out of our fear and our vulnerability; we can only feel our way beyond these beliefs.

Our real sense of security comes from our knowing, at a deep feeling level, that the Universe is a truly safe place and that each of us is totally safe in It. Our sense of security increases every time we expand our vision, open our hearts more and reclaim more of our power. As our self-empowerment grows, our investment of power in the physical world diminishes proportionately.

Eventually we reach a point where we know, with absolute certainty, that our open-hearted connection with our God presence, our Oneness, is not only real, it is primary in our lives. From this place of knowing, we realize that we create money not to make us feel secure, but as a way to express the power of our God presence. And we trust that the physical world we live in will always mirror our ever-expanding vision, our continually opening hearts and our increasing empowerment.

This is what true security is all about.

9

INTEGRITY

Integrity is defined as the state of being whole. We feel our integrity when we feel our connection to the Wholeness.

A person whose heart is open and who feels connected to others is coming from a place of integrity. As long as the person's heart continues to stay open and the feeling of connection is sustained, the person remains in integrity.

There probably is no personal quality that is more admired and appreciated than integrity. We each have a deep yearning to reconnect, at the heart level, with all other hearts.

The beauty of integrity lies in its all-inclusiveness. Problems arise from exclusion, not from inclusion. Whatever we open our hearts to is no longer a source of difficulty or challenge for us. Integrity is expanded in our lives as we little by little open our hearts wider and invite more hearts to connect with ours.

We cannot force ourselves to expand our integrity. But we can notice when our sense of self seems limited and our connection to others feels disrupted. Seeing ourselves as separate physical beings precludes our reaching beyond the physical boundaries of each of us. The perception that we are separate encourages us to focus on our differences—such as in skin color, religious background, amount of wealth—and to try to disconnect ourselves from the feelings and thoughts of others.

However, since we are each part of the Wholeness, we do in fact feel what others feel and know what they know. Any attempt to disconnect from these feelings and thoughts requires that we repress or block our feelings and that we close off our connection with our Wholeness.

We are so conditioned to see others as separate from us and, more than that, in competition with us, that we look for ways to withhold from them. What we don't realize is that when we withhold from others, we withhold from ourselves. This is also how we create shortage in our lives.

By heightening our awareness that we have chosen to see ourselves as separate and in competition, we reach the realization that we have created a shortage of money for ourselves as a way of withholding money from others. Out of this realization can then come the willingness to reconnect with our Wholeness and experience the abundance that is available to us all.

A word of counsel about this process: Whenever we notice that our sense of self is limited and we feel that our integrity is diminished, it is important that we accept this state as being perfect just the way it is. For judging ourselves only serves to further repress our feelings and more tightly close our hearts, which further disconnects us from our Wholeness.

When we are ready, we will feel the inspiration to open our hearts, and with that opening will come the natural desire to share generously with others. When our hearts are open, we know that sharing what we have is fun and inspires others to share what they have; that being generous to another is being generous to ourselves; and that the more we add to our circle, the more there is for everyone.

INTEGRITY

As our integrity expands, so does the abundance that flows from our sharing, our generosity and our mutual support. There is no limit to the expansion of our open hearts, and there is no limit to the ways money and all aspects of our material world can be used to express our open-hearted love for one another.

10

MONEY AND POWER

Poverty and homelessness have been with us for a long time. But it is only in recent years that the number of people experiencing these conditions has increased dramatically. Furthermore, many people are coming to the realization that the things they considered to be financially secure—long-term jobs, stable rates of interest, savings to support retirement—are no longer dependable. While upward mobility was the dream, for many people, downward mobility has become the reality.

This has led more and more of us to question our view of money as power, and to take another look at the relative value we have placed on money—and on ourselves.

Money has no inherent power, even though in many societies, including ours, we make believe that it does. Dollar bills, certificates of deposit, stocks, bonds and titles to real estate are just pieces of paper. Yet many of us still prefer to see money and its equivalents as having tremendous power, and ourselves as having little or none. Consequently, we devote a large portion of our lives to obtaining and accumulating money while we pay little attention to ourselves and each other.

When we are ready to look beyond money for the source of our power, we will begin to see where the real power lies. The first step is reminding ourselves that we bought into the idea that money contains power, and second, reminding ourselves that we cannot give away our power; it remains with us no matter what we believe. Dollar bills and their equivalents do not plan cities or design clothing. It is our conceptual, creative and artistic power that enables us to do these things. It is also our power that creates the money to construct the cities we plan and to build the facilities to manufacture the clothes we design.

Once we are willing to take money out of the lead position and place ourselves there, we are ready for the next step—recognizing that our power comes from beyond the physical, is unlimited in supply, and is equally accessible to all.

The concept of equal accessibility, or equality, can be a difficult one to accept in our hierarchical society, with its deep-seated beliefs that some people are more valuable than others and that "getting ahead" is a sacred right. The practical problem for those of us holding onto the hierarchical system is that by not seeing everyone as equally deserving of support, we automatically see ourselves as unworthy of that support, although we may not be aware of the connection.

Experiencing the fullness of ourselves requires that we support the same experience in others. Since each of us is the Wholeness, we can only enjoy and appreciate this Wholeness when it includes everyone and everything. This means that at any time and for any reason we believe someone is not entitled to share fully in the abundance of our Universe, we can benefit from opening our hearts to the "unworthy" person. For the unworthy person is always ourself, and when our heart opens, it opens to both.

The moment of recognition that our power lies in our open heart is an extraordinary moment. It inspires increased dedication to the process of feeling our feelings even more deeply, opening our hearts even more fully, and connecting with our God presence, the Wholeness, with even greater trust.

As we become more comfortable with our power and allow ourselves to reclaim more of it, we realize that it is our access to unlimited abundance. We also realize that the material world is an outgrowth of this power; it was never the source of it.

These realizations, in turn, increase our comfort with and our confidence in our God presence. With our willingness to acknowledge our own God presence, we naturally find ourselves seeing and feeling this God presence in others. Our world then becomes a great playground for God beings. And money, infused with our God presence, becomes just another toy we have to play with.

11

THE VALUE
OF CIRCUMSTANCES

L ife is essentially a series of relationships that take place in settings that we call circumstances. As varied as these circumstances may be, the purpose of each and every one of them is always the same: to arouse feelings.

Why? Because we are essentially feeling beings and it is through our feelings that we connect with the energy that sustains us and is our power. It is through our feelings that we connect with our God presence, our Oneness.

We are very powerful beings, and when we open ourselves fully to our feelings, we access our full power. The wisest part of us knows this and thus directs us to those circumstances that will arouse the most intense feelings and thus give us access to the greatest amount of our power.

Our willingness to focus on our feelings rather than on the circumstances that arouse the feelings is a heroic choice, particularly at those times when the circumstances seem so compelling. Wars, earthquakes, bankruptcy, child abuse, divorce, illness, poverty, death—all seem preeminently worthy of our full attention.

Such events are all the more compelling because we have been trained for generations to view the circumstances as significant and our feelings about them as inconsequential. Furthermore, we have been diligently taught to judge each and every circumstance as good or bad, right or wrong.

Shifting our focus away from the circumstances and to the feelings the circumstances evoke only proves its value when we do it. The choice to feel our feelings calls not only for commitment but for persistence. Since we have so many judgments about these circumstances, each time we feel our feelings and open our hearts a little more, another judgment surfaces to open the energy around.

What does it mean to open the energy around a judgment? It means being willing to feel the feeling separate from the judgment that is repressing it, and then being willing to open our hearts to the feeling. The most practical way to accomplish this is by going through the three steps of the Feeling Exercise.

In the same way that we were taught to believe that certain circumstances were wrong and bad, we were told that feeling our intense feelings was difficult and uncomfortable. In truth, these feelings are just pure loving vibrations eager for a reconnection with us. And we can take all the time we wish to connect with them. In fact, the process works most effectively when we take small steps consistently, and allow the reconnection to occur gradually.

Every circumstance we find ourselves in gives us another opportunity to open our energy fields and our hearts a little more, and to reclaim a little more of our power. For many of us, the circumstances surrounding money arouse some of the most intense, and therefore the most power-laden, feelings of all. When we trust in the process enough to keep our focus on it, we not only notice that our relationship with money becomes simpler and more joyful, we strengthen our conviction that we are the creators of our unlimited abundance.

12

"IN GOD
WE TRUST"

It was not on a whim that the founders of our country chose to have inscribed on every dollar bill the statement "In God We Trust." They understood that our relationship with money derives from our relationship with God, and that if we did not trust in God, our Oneness, our relationship with money would reflect that lack of trust.

Money is neutral. It moves in our lives in accordance with the flow of energy in and around us. When we are experiencing any distortion or block in the flow of energy in and around us, money will follow the same pattern.

The clarity, ease and fullness of our relationship with money mirrors the clarity, ease and fullness of our relationship with our God presence, our Oneness. Because money is a derivative experience, we cannot have a more satisfying or fulfilling relationship with money than we do with that from which money derives.

There is a simple yet profound exercise that can tell us a great deal about the quality of our relationship with our God presence. Practiced consistently, it can help us to enrich all of our relationships, including those with money.

THE MIRROR EXERCISE

Stand or sit in front of a mirror and look at yourself until you feel love for yourself. At first, you're likely to notice things about yourself that you don't love—physical characteristics as well as other aspects of yourself that you judge as being less than perfect. Whatever you don't love about yourself will come into your awareness as you continue looking in the mirror.

This is an exercise in perseverance, but as you stay with it, you'll find that your ability to accept yourself just the way you are increases each time you are willing to come face to face with yourself. Your heart does open a little more and you do connect a little more deeply to your God presence and to the love that is your essence.

Even for those who are able to see and feel the love, the God presence, at times, there are other times when the connection may seem to be broken, when we are not at peace with the Oneness. The solution then is to first do the Feeling Exercise until the peacefulness returns.

We are all so used to being in our minds and using our intellects to guide us through our day, that placing our focus and trust in our feelings, and through them connecting to our Oneness, is not something we do easily. It is true that it takes practice—not because being in our hearts and feeling our feelings is unnatural to us, but because we have established such strong reliance on our conscious minds. We have come to place our trust in our intellects rather than in our Oneness.

If we look at all of the sophisticated ways that people deal with money—such as arbitrage, commodity and currency trading, and leveraged buy-outs—we can see just how far we have gone to make money an intellectual experience. In essence, what has happened is that money has ceased being a heart-based experience. And when the heart is closed, we feel the discomfort in our relationship with money.

This might seem like an oversimplification, but it is not. Love, God, the Wholeness, Oneness, harmony, peacefulness, trust—all of these are simple concepts. They are so powerful because they are simple, and because each and every one of them is a term that relates to a fully open heart.

Some might ask how anyone can have a successful relationship with money without at least some knowledge of the basics of finances. There are a number of answers to that question.

Most people learn fairly early in their lives the rudimentary aspects of personal finances, such as balancing a checkbook and budgeting income. When something beyond this kind of simple financial management is involved, there are accountants and other professionals to advise us.

The more important issue is the attitude we hold when we approach financial matters. Whenever there is an attempt to have a successful relationship with money based on mastering the ways money moves in the physical world, we are approaching the situation backwards. No matter how sophisticated a person's approach to money is, money cannot provide a benefit greater than the consciousness of the one devising the relationship.

Secondly, intellectual relationships are always of limited value, since the heart must be closed to some extent when the approach is with the conscious mind. This is not to say that large amounts of money cannot be made. We are looking at the *quality* of the relationship, and it is the amount of heart energy that determines the true quality of any relationship.

Let's look at this another way. As we know, money, in and of itself, has no power. A dollar bill will not prepare a dinner or plant a garden. People do these things.

There are many different ways to cook a meal or grow flowers and vegetables. When these or any other activities, including managing our financial affairs, are done with a fully open heart, the experience for the person performing the task, as well as for everyone else involved in it, is of the highest quality. The open-heart energy that is transmitted is not only powerful; it is empowering, it is nurturing, it is satisfying. It is the essence of unconditional love.

When we honor, trust and enjoy our open hearts, we assure ourselves the most fulfilling relationship with our Oneness. It is then that our relationship with money functions as successfully as the founders of our country intended.

13

THE ROLES
WE PLAY

We are not the roles that we play in life. We are not children, parents, brothers, sisters, teachers, students, musicians, authors, presidents, cab drivers and all the other roles we see played out constantly. We also are not the qualities that we display, such as smart, shallow, meticulous, careless, generous or stingy.

We play these roles and display these qualities in the same way that an actor assumes a persona in a play or film. And, like a good actor, we play our roles so well that we convince everyone that we are the person whose role we are playing. We even believe it ourselves.

We also accept, with equally strong conviction, the roles others have chosen to play. And we respond to them just as if the roles they are playing are who they really are.

What is the purpose of this remarkable charade? Put most simply, we come into this life to expand our consciousness through our experiences. In order to do this, we have to fully integrate the experiences and the beliefs that accompany them at a deep feeling level. And this means we have to allow ourselves to accept totally that our experiences and beliefs are real.

Paradoxically, we cannot fully integrate our experiences and thus expand our consciousness until we recognize what we have done: accepted our role selves as our real selves. What is fascinating about this process is that the first stage of total acceptance of our experiences as real sets in motion the second stage of awakening to the truth.

The way the process works is that our experiences compel us to confront, at a feeling level, the roles that we are projecting. If we avoid feeling these feelings, the constriction of energy produces pain. Eventually, the pain intensifies until we see that the only solution is to begin the process of opening our energy fields and reconnecting to our feelings, which not only expands our consciousness but puts us in touch with the true power of our being.

In moving through this process, it is important to appreciate the intensity of the energy that is involved in the roles and dramas we chose to take on. As children, many of us encountered scenarios that we interpreted as assaults on our freedom to fully and freely express ourselves, and we became angry and resentful at this apparently blatant lack of love and support. However, because we were taught that these responsive emotions were unacceptable, we suppressed them. As the years went by, the anger and resentment grew in intensity. Still, the fear of responding as well as the memory of being unloved and unsupported discouraged us from approaching these seemingly volatile emotions.

As the process of awakening commences and the love that is the energy in these emotions insists on expressing, we experience a most dynamic conflict within us. Our essence, who we really are, which is pure love, comes face to face with the role that we have been playing. Our real self encounters our role self, as well as the belief—so strong after so many years—that we were wronged and are entitled to retribution.

As the awakening process continues, we begin to appreciate that the only reason that we are still resisting the love that is literally crying out for expression is that we are not yet willing to release that vow we made to ourselves when we were children that we would someday get even with those whom we perceived were unloving toward us.

However, things *are* different now. We are no longer children. We are beginning to see through the roles we and the members of our family and community have been playing, and to accept that all of us have been volunteers in this very challenging but very dynamic and transformative process.

We are also beginning to know that the love within us is so powerful and relentless in its drive to prevail, that it will eventually succeed. It will succeed all the sooner when we are willing to let go of that vow we made to get even with those we believe hurt us. As our desire for revenge dissolves, we make way for the full and free expression of our true and natural role—that of unconditional lover.

14

THE GIFT
OF COMPASSION

Reaching a state of compassion is the ultimate gift we give ourselves as human beings. It is knowing and feeling that all power is within us and that none is vested outside of us—neither in material things nor in the circumstances of our lives. Compassion comes from loving ourselves so completely that we see and feel others only through that love. In a state of compassion, Oneness is our reality.

Many people confuse compassion with concern or worry. To the extent that these emotions are present, we can be sure we have vested power in some circumstance outside of us, and our capacity to feel compassion is diminished.

Whatever we experience is always a reflection of the state of our own consciousness. When we feel worried or concerned about someone, it has nothing to do with the other person. It is always our own state with which we are resonating. If we are free of worry and concern, another person cannot stimulate these emotions in us.

Very often, a person who is reaching out for support will try to convince us that the circumstances surrounding her are real and that she is powerless and a victim. If she is successful in getting us to accept that she is really separate from her God presence, the Oneness, we both journey further into the belief of separateness, powerlessness and victimhood.

An example is a person begging on a street corner. Typically, someone passing by accepts this display of poverty as real and sympathizes with the beggar. But sympathy is the opposite of compassion. Sympathy accepts the separateness and powerlessness as real. Compassion *knows* we are never separate or powerless. Compassion allows us to connect directly with the God presence of the beggar, feel his true power, and trust in his choice to fully experience the role of beggar. We are then free to decide, without the sense of obligation that accompanies sympathy, whether or not to offer him material support.

When we feel compassion, we are sending out the most powerful love and support available. Our deep trust in the unconditional love and support of the Universe connects directly with the recipient's heart and God presence. The recipient is then in a position to access this enormous love and power that, in fact, has always been available.

There is nothing more valuable we can aspire to achieve than a state of compassion. This deeply loving state embodies Universal Principles in action. The sender feels the great sense of empowerment from her most generous gift, and the recipient feels the great sense of empowerment from having his true self acknowledged and supported.

15

WHERE TRUE
WEALTH LIES

As we move toward the twenty-first century, more and more of us are coming to appreciate that the broader our vision and the wider open our hearts, the richer our lives become. And the more we connect with our Wholeness, at a deep feeling level, the more we allow the unlimitedness that we are to support us.

There is never a shortage of support. What there is is less than total willingness and readiness to open to all of the support that is always available to us.

Money literally flows into our lives only to the extent that we allow it to. Our view of life, ourselves and others always determines the size of the flow. As our view of life, ourselves and others expands, so does our relationship with money.

Remember, money is a derivative. Money has no value, no power, in and of itself. It relies for all of its significance on the person who is relating to it. When we relate to money with an open heart, with love, integrity, generosity and compassion, it takes on these qualities from us.

When our sense of ourselves is very limited, when we are self-critical and judgmental, we infuse money with qualities that are constrictive and unloving. Money then acts accordingly in our lives. Until we feel more love for ourselves, we do not allow others to be generous to us.

Attempts to stimulate the flow of money by becoming very active—such as working hard for long hours—only serve to transmit the attributes inherent in this work style into our relationship with money. Hard work and long hours create fatigue, frustration, irritability and very often resentment. When these qualities are present, at the feeling level, regardless of how we attempt to characterize them differently, they do infuse our relationship with money.

Thoughts about money move us into an intellectual relationship with money. Money filled with head energy isn't much fun. It is only when we reach a state of open-heartedness with money that the fun begins.

What does it take for each of us to reach this state? It is a very personal and subjective process that is unique to each of us. But the process is essentially one of opening our hearts little by little and feeling love first for ourselves and then for each person to whom our hearts are closed.

Abundance *is* the natural state of the Universe. We access the abundance through our open hearts. We have all tried many other methods of accessing abundance and have learned individually and collectively of the shortcomings of each of these other methods. Our explorations have, however, been purposeful in that they have motivated us to finally look in the place where our true wealth is located.

Life is essentially a simple experience. We have chosen to see it as complex because we are on a journey to gain the experiences that derive from creating this complexity. We know that the greater the variety of circumstances we create, the greater the variety of feelings we arouse. And the more extensive the range of feelings we bring to the surface and are willing to feel, the more power we reclaim and the more expanded our consciousness becomes—which is what we came here to do.

So everything is purposeful and perfect. When we can accept the perfection of this process, we can align with the process and support it rather than resist or retard it. We can also remind ourselves that even our resistance serves the purpose of intensifying the feelings that we will connect with eventually.

Our open hearts contain not only our wealth, but everything we require to enjoy our wealth. They contain the trust that allows us to open even more to the Wholeness of which we are all a part. Our open hearts contain the gratitude that lets us appreciate all of the abundance we already have. They contain the generosity that encourages us to share all of our expanding abundance fully and freely with others. And they contain the absolute knowledge that our open hearts *are* our true wealth, and that increasing our wealth simply means opening our hearts wider.

PART TWO

GROUNDING
THE VISION

16

ALIGNMENT
WITH PURPOSE

We each have a general, overall purpose for our life, and that is to feel our connection to and expand our God presence, our Oneness, on the planet and in the Universe. Out of this general purpose that we all share come our individual purposes.

How do we each discover our individual purpose? The first step is to align with our larger purpose, which means connecting with it at a feeling level. We do this by opening our hearts and feeling the power of our Oneness. Once we feel our power through an open heart, we are ready to attune to our individual purpose.

Gaining clarity about our individual purpose is no different from gaining clarity about anything else. It happens when we allow our thoughts to flow through our minds freely and without conscious-mind intervention. When the flow of thoughts through our minds is totally free, what is really flowing through is Infinite Intelligence. It is in this state of mind that we connect with our purpose.

One point about purpose that is useful to note: We may compose a beautifully worded and poetic statement of purpose, but if we do not connect with it at a feeling level, our statement of purpose is just an intellectual exercise. How do we recognize our true purpose? By noticing how we feel. When we feel the inspiration of our stated purpose infusing our being, we know we have connected to our true purpose.

The value of purpose is that it is such an extraordinarily simple way of focusing our energy. The depth and intensity of the focus depends upon the depth and intensity of the feeling that our purpose inspires. Therefore, we are wise not only to be sensitive to our purpose, but to open to it at deeper and deeper levels.

As we continue with the process of opening to our purpose and connecting to the fullness of ourselves, we feel the expansiveness of this process push up against the boundaries of our current limited definition of ourselves. The reluctance we feel to support the expansion is based, in part, on our loyalty to the status quo.

Loyalty is a most significant issue for most of us. We feel loyalty not only to our families, regardless of how unloving we may have perceived them to be, but to friends, school, religion, country. And each one to whom we feel loyal had a part in helping us develop our present definition of ourselves.

Staying connected with our purpose and feeling inspired by it is one of the ways we transcend the boundaries of our limited definition of self. It is how we move beyond our loyalty to the status quo to the fullness and power of who we really are.

As our sense of purpose expands and inspires us even more, we find that all of life becomes filled with a sense of purpose. It is then that our relationship with money takes on the inspiration of our purpose and that money begins to move in our lives in more purposeful, inspired ways.

Whenever we are feeling confused, alone or unsupported, we can be sure we have disconnected from our stated purpose. Taking the time to reconnect with the inspiration of our purpose is most valuable and puts us back in the process of opening our hearts and feeling the power of our God presence. As this happens, our relationship with money is once again inspired by our renewed sense of purpose.

17

UNCONDITIONAL
LOVE

We feel our connection with our God presence, the Wholeness, through our open hearts. The more open our hearts, the deeper our connection to our God presence and the more powerful we feel.

The justification for closing our hearts is the belief that someone or something is not perfect just the way it is. The result is conditional love. The more we value the condition, the more completely we close our hearts and the less powerful we feel.

Conditional love is essentially loving someone only after the person meets our conditions. These conditions are so important to us that they are literally preconditions to opening ourselves to the feeling of love in us and allowing this love to connect with the love in another.

What we commonly call an emotion—such as anger, sadness, elation—is an interpretation of a feeling by the conscious mind. The interpretation is, in effect, a condition that distorts the feeling and keeps us from feeling it fully and freely with our hearts wide open.

A condition is a judgment. When we judge a person as not being perfect just the way he is, we justify withholding love from that person. We invariably see the judgment as being the result of something the other person has said or done. What we fail to see is that it is our mind's interpretation of the words spoken or the act performed that gives rise to the judgment or condition.

As we expand our awareness of who we really are, we recognize that the condition is a totally subjective experience on our part and has nothing at all to do with the behavior of another. We are never really at the effect of another. We are never really victims. However, having been carefully taught that we are, we dutifully make believe that we are and continue the game of conditional love.

Our presence on this planet is an opportunity to open the energy around all of our many conditions. To take advantage of this opportunity, we can remember that we chose these conditions. We chose the parents, siblings, relatives, friends and associates who would generate the precise conditions that we now find so challenging.

Once we accept this broader view, we can move to the next step, which is opening our hearts and feeling our feelings fully and freely without the intervention of the conscious mind. As we continue in this process, we lose more and more of our investment in our conditions. Our love becomes increasingly unconditional, which means the power in the love becomes more available to us.

In connecting with our true power, we automatically place money in a new perspective. We know that money, like everything else in the material world, is an outgrowth of the state of our consciousness. We know that money flows freely in our lives when we allow it to. We also know that when money isn't flowing freely, we have given importance to some condition.

Unconditional love is the real game of life. It is the way we connect to the power that we truly are. It is also the doorway to our natural environment of inner peace, mutual support, joyfulness and abundance.

18

MUTUAL
SUPPORT

The concept of mutual support derives from our true state of being, which is a state of Oneness. Giving and receiving support lovingly and generously is natural to us. It aligns perfectly with our purpose of feeling and expanding our Oneness. Since we feel our Oneness when we open our hearts, being mutually supportive is simpler than we realize.

It is interesting, then, that we have chosen to live in a capitalistic society that encourages us to compete with one another and to treat each other as adversaries. Being competitive is unnatural to us and requires many years of careful and consistent training beginning at an early age. The main focus of this training is keeping our hearts closed and repressing our feelings, which shuts us off from our Oneness. That we suffer so much fear and stress in our society is hardly surprising.

Despite what appears to be an illogical and misdirected choice to live in such a society, there is perfection in this choice. For it gives us the opportunity to open our hearts *within the system*, and thus to expand the power of unconditional love and mutual support. This expansion of power is then available to everyone to simplify and ease our lives.

Being mutually supportive is not only natural to us, we thrive on it.

Mutual support is nurturing, enlivening and inspiring, and leads to wonderfully creative activities.

When feelings of unconditional love and mutual support flow freely within a group—and a group consists of two or more people—the participants find that they can easily manage any and all problems that arise. For love is the most powerful force in the Universe, and the consistent focus of unconditional love by those in an environment of mutual support can transform anything.

What we call problems are just circumstances that we have vested our power in. We then feel at the effect of our own power. When we are willing to accept what we have done, we can reclaim our power by opening our hearts.

With all of the emphasis in our society on individualism and competition, we have a constant reminder of the importance of balancing our intensely adversarial way of life with relationships that are mutually supportive and unconditionally loving, and that encourage us to stay connected to the true power of our Oneness.

In a mutually supportive environment, keeping our hearts open is easy and fun. We soon recognize how satisfying this kind of environment is, and we seek to recreate it wherever we are.

19

GRATITUDE

Compared with most people in the world, those reading this book are appreciably better off. We have more freedom, more opportunities and more material wealth than just about anyone on earth.

Yet our underlying emotion is one of insecurity and fear. We believe that there is not enough for everyone and that only those who are aggressive and competitive will win out. Many of us also believe that the future is bringing even fewer opportunities, and that with more and more countries looking to raise their standards of living, our own standard of living will most certainly have to diminish.

This general acceptance of a world of shortage results in a paradoxical response. Instead of appreciating all that so many of us do have, we take for granted what we have and worry endlessly about what we do not have. In addition, we act in ways that are very illogical and imprudent for people who accept that shortage is a fact of life. We run up large debts and borrow heavily against those things we do have—our houses or our incomes.

What is most devastating about this irrational response is the depressed feeling quality that comes in its wake. Many people are exhausted from fighting this battle known as "keeping ahead."

There is a simple solution. It is the willingness to feel gratitude for all that we presently have. And we have so much. The least of it is that which we tend to value the most—our material possessions.

While it is valuable to feel gratitude for the least significant material possession we have, the power of the process escalates as we feel gratitude for our more significant gifts, beginning with life itself. When we are really honest with ourselves, we know what is truly important in our lives. At our deepest level, we do appreciate who we really are. We appreciate the power that resides in us—our God presence, which is always there waiting for us to acknowledge It and, more than that, to honor It.

Gratitude is an aspect of love. It is a powerful focus that cuts through the confusion and chaos of our misperception of life as a scary struggle for survival and puts us in touch with the unlimited abundance that is always present. Whenever we allow ourselves to feel gratitude for anything, our hearts open and we connect a little more deeply to our God presence and to our power.

From a most practical standpoint, why have anything if, when having it, we deny ourselves the greatest benefit we can possibly derive from it— the feeling of gratitude?

20

TWO LEVELS OF
CONSCIOUSNESS

We experience life at two levels of consciousness. One is with the conscious mind. The other is with Mind as the God presence, or Infinite Intelligence.

The conscious mind, or intellect, is the part of us that we use to assemble data and figure things out. Our conscious minds rely solely on the physical world for information. Decisions made with our conscious minds are limited to what we can see, hear, touch, taste and smell.

Our Mind with a capital "M" is the part of us that sees beyond the physical to the broader perspective and understands that everything and everyone in our lives is purposeful and perfect just the way it is. Our Mind is all knowing, all wise, loves us unconditionally and supports us totally.

Our Mind is often referred to as our intuition, our inner knowing. It is always present and active in us. Although we often choose not to open our awarenes to It, our Mind is always guiding us through our lives.

When we choose to use our conscious minds to solve problems, make decisions and evaluate circumstances, we are choosing to block our awareness of our Mind as the God presence. We then fall prey to limited beliefs and a narrow vision, which leads us to feel powerless and fearful, and we tend to grab at whatever is available to make us feel stronger and more secure. From this limited perspective, the only things that seem real are aspects of the physical world—money, possessions and positions of influence.

Interestingly, the more material support we rely on, the more insecure we feel; and the weaker we feel, the more material support we believe we need. It is a rapidly descending spiral that is accompanied by a growing sense of vulnerability and insecurity, an increasingly tightly shut heart, and more and more pain.

As inevitable and irreversible as this downward spiral seems to someone who is having such an experience, a shift in direction is always available. Infinite Intelligence is always there to guide us in expanding our vision and reclaiming our power.

How do we connect with this Greater Intelligence? The access point is our feelings. Whenever we are willing to feel our feelings and open our hearts, we connect with this most expansive energy.

Often we avoid feeling our feelings because we believe the process is too painful. Instead, we fall back on our training to use our intellects to solve problems, and we attempt to *understand* our feelings rather than feel them. This keeps the power in the feelings separate from us. Many of us are so sophisticated in using our conscious minds to avoid feeling our feelings that our intellects have, in effect, become defense mechanisms that we employ to keep our feelings at bay.

Our extensive use of our conscious minds in dealing with money tells us that we are feeling powerless, fearful and insecure. It also tells us that we have once again chosen the illusion of power of the conscious mind over the true power of Infinite Mind.

When we open our hearts enough to connect with our God presence, we do not feel the need to protect ourselves. The power inherent in this all-knowing, loving, supportive state fills us with a sense of peacefulness and allows money and all other gifts to flow through our lives freely, generously and naturally

21

THE POWER
OF PEACEFULNESS

Everything we see around us and how we experience it is always an outplaying of the state of our consciousness, not only individually but as part of the consciousness of the various groups to which we belong—family, community, state, nation, world and Universe. When the group consciousness has a very narrow focus, which is another way of describing a conscious-mind focus that is fear based, the circumstances that the group experiences can seem very frightening, chaotic and painful.

On the other hand, no matter how limited the focus of the group may be, each individual member is always free to choose Infinite Intelligence's broader perspective. The broader the perspective chosen, the less frightening, chaotic and painful will be this individual's experience with these same circumstances.

The purpose of circumstances, remember, is to arouse feelings so that they can be fully felt. Each time we align with this purpose, our experience with the circumstances of our lives becomes a little more peaceful. The greater our sense of peacefulness, the more our hearts open and the more we feel our Oneness. The power we feel from this process expresses itself as greater confidence in our natural state of peace, harmony and creativity.

The challenge to opening to our feelings and feeling them fully is our years of training and strong patterning to lead with our conscious minds. Our society is in such an advanced state of intellectual development that we have lived for many generations with great amounts of repressed feelings. These feelings are always trying to free themselves, but our patterns of repression keep them in check, although it requires great effort on our part.

One of the most self-supportive ways to approach this challenge is by learning to quiet our conscious minds through the practice of meditation. Meditation is simply a process of allowing our God presence to become more fully present in our lives.

Since our access to the God presence is through our feelings, the most efficient way to begin the meditation process is with the Feeling Exercise, repeating it as often as necessary to fully open our hearts. When our hearts are fully open, we feel peaceful. It is then that we are ready to enjoy the process of meditation or, in fact, any other activity.

In sports, athletes using innovative training techniques have demonstrated that when they increase their state of peacefulness, huge amounts of energy naturally flow through them and they are able to perform at their peak level of ability. The key to this new approach is the realization that peacefulness opens our energy fields and allows us to connect with our natural energy and inherent power.

For many years we have defined peacefulness in terms of weakness and passivity. From an expanded vantage point, it can be seen as the powerful state it truly is.

22

INSPIRATION

Inspiration is the spontaneous expression of love. It flows out of an open heart consciously connected to our Oneness. We sometimes confuse inspiration with excitement. However, they are really opposite states.

We seek excitement to distract us when our hearts are closed and we wish to avoid feeling feelings that are uncomfortable. We can watch a murder mystery on TV, bet on the horses, get drunk or take drugs.

In order for something to have the capacity to distract us, we must first vest it with importance. We literally give it power. In turn, we feel as though the same amount of power has left us. Thus, in order to make something exciting—that is, give it the power to distract us—we make ourselves seem weaker.

Inspiration, on the other hand, can only arise when we feel powerful. It springs from our willingness to feel all of our feelings and to fully open our hearts to them. When our hearts are open, we are connected to our Oneness, and inspiration flows freely and naturally.

Unlike excitement, inspiration requires no effort. Inspiration leaves us feeling energized and alive. Excitement often leaves us feeling tired, anxious about returning to a feeling that is uncomfortable, and drained of our power. When our conscious minds are active, we can be sure we are routed on the excitement-discomfort continuum, perpetually moving from one extreme to the other. Our time is spent craving excitement and desperately trying to escape discomfort.

We can, however, choose at any moment to still our minds, open our hearts and feel our connection to our Oneness. We then enjoy the peacefulness and spontaneity that give rise to inspiration, along with all the free-flowing love and creativity that accompany inspiration.

23

CREATIVITY

Our connection to our Oneness is our connection to our true creativity. We have within us all potential. We limit ourselves only by our beliefs that we are limited.

When we rely on our conscious minds to come up with ideas and develop solutions, we are choosing to bypass the avenue to our creativity. The intellect, which is only capable of drawing on past experiences and information that is stored in our individual memories, provides us with an infinitesimal part of the knowledge that is available to us.

The metaphor of the computer is so often used because it is so accurate. Our conscious minds are like computers that have stored in their memories a range of software programs. For all the wonderful capabilities computers have, they can only do what they have been programmed to do.

Creativity is the free flow of Universal Intelligence through our energy fields and our hearts, from and to the Oneness. Whatever unique talents, skills and experiences we have are our gift from and contribution to this Oneness.

Opening to and expressing our creativity calls for our willingness to fully and freely support, in love, everyone and everything. Creativity, by definition, means openness, expansion, total freedom. Beliefs, on the other hand, are always constrictive and thus block access to our creativity.

Take, as an example, an architect who is commissioned to design a building. If his belief is that he must outshine his competitors, make a lot of money for himself, or demonstrate how brilliant a designer he is, he will inhibit his true creativity.

This is not to imply that being competitive, making a lot of money or demonstrating brilliance is bad or wrong. It is just that these beliefs, which derive from a narrow sense of self, one that separates self from others, can only result in a product of limited creativity.

We can see from this example that society's definition of creativity and true creativity are quite different and consequently produce quite different results. What is missing from our traditional view is the awareness that each of us *is* the Wholeness and that our purpose is to enjoy the richness and unlimited potential of our Wholeness and to support Its full expression.

Many of us are beginning to realize just how limited are our beliefs about who we are, what life is about and what our relationship with the Universe and each other is. We seem to see ourselves as wind-up dolls the size of ants plodding through a maze the size of a shoebox. It is our sense of ourselves as so small and valueless that discourages us from eagerly expressing our unique talents and participating fully in life.

Our reluctance to see ourselves as the powerful beings we are brings up a most significant principle. How we perceive ourselves is the vantage point from which we interpret life. When we see ourselves as meaningless and inconsequential, we see others the same way, they see us that way, and life indeed appears to have no meaning.

The solution comes in allowing our sense of ourselves to expand until it encompasses the Wholeness that we truly are. Then, when the channel between us and the Wholeness is open and clear, we connect to the unlimited potential and boundless creativity that is really just love flowing freely and fully.

A simple way to know how much love is flowing in and out of us is to do the Mirror Exercise. When we feel love for what we see in the mirror, we know that our channel to the Oneness is open and that love, and thus creativity, is freely flowing.

What happens when we connect with our creativity? We simply allow it to flow, knowing that our creativity always contains the Infinite Intelligence to express perfectly. A vision is painted on a canvas; a melody is played on a musical instrument; ideas are formulated into words on paper. Creativity is the Oneness expressing through us, bringing aliveness and fulfillment in Its wake.

24

CORE ISSUES

The process of opening our hearts and connecting to our Oneness brings with it many challenges, among them what I refer to as core issues. As challenging as these issues may be, it is our willingness to make peace with them that enables our hearts to open sufficiently wide to allow in all the creative potential and abundance our Oneness holds for us.

What are core issues? They are the unresolved issues we have involving parents, siblings, relatives, caretakers, authority figures and others who were significant in our infancy and childhood years. These are the people who taught us what life was about, who modeled for us how we were to behave, and who showed us the ways we could expect others to behave. They are the ones who molded our beliefs, which became so much a part of us that they now govern our approach to everyone and everything.

In essence, our issue with these key people is that, as we interpreted their attitude and behavior toward us, they were not consistently unconditionally loving and supportive. They may have acted uncaring or even cruel. And we are still angry and resentful about it. In fact, we are determined to get even with them and with those people we have chosen to represent them.

The way we interpreted the words and actions of those who raised us led us to respond with emotions that we later defined as anger, fear, sadness or guilt. At the time, however, we were not supported in honoring these intense feeling responses. We were not given the opportunity to feel them fully and to connect with the power in them. Far from it. We were taught to repress these feelings and thus cut ourselves off from our power. And we have continued this repression into adulthood so that we now have a veritable storehouse of unfelt feelings within us that has left us feeling powerless.

Our core issues deeply influence every area of our lives. They not only affect us, they affect everyone with whom we live, work and interact. And although it takes a great deal of focused attention, commitment and perseverance to open the energy around these core issues, until we are willing to do so, we deny ourselves the gift of knowing what a full and free expression of self feels like and how powerful we really are. Furthermore, these core issues have such huge amounts of energy locked up in them that until we are willing to free this energy, we will experience increasing stress and discomfort.

While the challenge to feel these intense energies fully may seem great and sometimes more than we are able to handle, there is an equivalently large payoff in doing so. For when we do free these energies by feeling and opening our hearts to them, we not only notice a significant reduction in stress and discomfort, we also notice an increase in our personal power.

Central to the efficient opening of this vast storehouse of compacted energy is our willingness to keep in our conscious awareness our most basic desire—to love and to be loved unconditionally. Equally important to keep in our awareness is the truth that each of us contains within us the capacity to give this unconditional love to ourselves. When we keep a consistent focus on these basic truths, we simplify the process and avoid being overwhelmed by the power in our repressed feelings.

We further support ourselves by looking at core issues from a broader perspective. From this more expansive view, we see that we agreed to come into this life to take on the precise experiences and the beliefs that go with them for the purpose of eventually opening up these intense energies and reclaiming as our own the power we locked in them.

Once we make a commitment to this process, everything in our lives opens up to support us. And we realize that the whole Universe mirrors our insatiable desire to love and be loved unconditionally.

Our parents and all the other people in our formative years who taught us what to believe and whose behavior we modeled remain our partners on our journey to satisfy this desire. As long as we blame and resent them and avoid feeling our feelings toward them, they mirror our withholding of unconditional love from them. However, they stand ready to mirror back to us our open-hearted, unconditional love for them so that together, and only together, we can find the deep peace and unlimited power that is waiting patiently inside of us.

25

MONEY
AND CORE ISSUES

In a society where money is such a dominant component, it becomes an instructional device to teach us what we have come here to learn. Money is particularly useful in attracting our attention to our core issues and, through the feelings contained in these core issues, in connecting us to our true power.

My own experiences as well as those of the large number of people who attend my workshops have demonstrated that challenges around money present themselves relentlessly until we open our hearts to these core issues. I can add that those of us who have stayed with the process for a reasonable period have come to the same conclusion: the more we open our hearts, the more powerful we feel and the more certainty we have of the unconditionally loving and supportive nature of the Universe.

To understand how money and core issues interrelate, we'll look at some specific Universal Principles, starting with the principle that abundance is the natural state of the Universe. The corollary to this principle is that if anyone is experiencing less than total abundance in each and every aspect of his life, it means that he is literally pushing abundance away.

This principle reminds us that it takes an activist position to keep money out; that when our resistance lowers, money flows in. So when money or anything else that can be supportive of us isn't present in our lives, we can be sure we are in a state of active resistance, although we may not be aware that we are.

There are many aspects of ourselves that exist concurrently. Not all of these aspects are in our conscious awareness at all times. In fact, most of the time, most of what is going on in our lives is not in our conscious awareness. Therefore, it is usually a less than conscious part of us that is doing the resisting, the pushing away.

How do we become aware of what we are unconsciously resisting? The answer is simple. All we need to do is look at the result we are achieving. For we always project outside of us a precise picture of what is going on inside.

Take as an example someone who is having difficulty paying her rent. What this situation often reveals is that, on an unconscious level, the tenant is withholding love and support from her landlord because her landlord represents a core person from her past.

The landlord also represents a part of herself from which she is withholding love and support. This stems from the fact that we always embody the core people in our lives. In other words, we identify with these core people at the same time that we try to treat them as separate from us.

Recognizing that each of us is always the core person we are still angry at or resentful of is a big and most valuable step to take. Once that step is taken, it is easier to accept the basic simplicity of the process of opening our hearts to our core issues.

It becomes even easier when we realize that we do not have to go rummaging into the past to make peace with our core issues. As interesting as the details surrounding our core issues may be, we do not need to delve into them. We don't have to know what parent or authority figure our land-lord represents. We don't need to know what childhood event is connected to our present challenging circumstance with money. In fact, attempts to analyze these core issues and try to make sense of them is counterproductive, for it puts us in our heads and takes us out of our hearts.

The way we open the energy around the core issues in our lives comes down to this elemental procedure: As soon as we notice any discomfort, we know that we are suppressing a feeling that is holding energy within it. We are ready for the Feeling Exercise. This simple exercise guides us in, first, feeling the feeling and the energy within it without paying any attention to the people or circumstances involved; second, opening our hearts and feeling love for the feeling and for the energy within the feeling; and third, feeling love for ourselves.

In terms of money and the principle of abundance, when we open our hearts to the core issues in our lives, we begin to move from a state of resistance into a state of openness. We also free up energy, which then becomes available to inspire our creativity, to deepen our appreciation of our Oneness, and to strengthen our natural desire to love and support one another.

A word to prepare you for this process: It does not go in a straight upward direction. There are times when we open up a great deal and release large amounts of energy; there are times when we open only imperceptibly; and there are times when we close down. If we were to graph the progress of someone who is consistent in his focus, we would see a steadily rising line with periodic dips.

This brings us to another principle that comes into play around core issues, and that is the principle of nonjudgment, with its corollary of forgiveness. This principle applies both to our current relationships and circumstances as well as to the people and events of our childhood. And since we always embody within us anyone we have feelings about, it also applies to ourselves.

Whenever we judge any circumstance or any person, including ourselves, for failing to fulfill our expectations or to perform according to our standards, we close our energy fields and our hearts. This puts us in a state of resistance where we push away support. Until we are willing to open our hearts to our judgments, we block our access to the loving support and natural abundance that is all around us.

Core issues can carry very intense feelings and thus a great deal of energy within them. Opening to these feelings and to this intense energy is sometimes more than we alone can handle—even if we try opening to just a small amount at a time, which is the wise approach. The solution comes from following another principle—the principle of mutual support.

There is in existence a large network of mutual support groups that meet, usually, on a weekly basis in local communities (see "Joining a Mutual Support Group" on page 191 for details). The purpose of these groups is to create an environment of unconditional love and mutual support where people not only can enjoy that environment, but also can gain the support they need when they are opening their hearts to their core issues.

Since all energy in the Universe is love, love is literally all around us. We either open to love or close ourselves off from it. Whenever we open ourselves to love, it flows in from all sources and in all forms.

As we open our hearts, we feel the fullness of ourselves and the extraordinary power of our God presence. And we know, deep down inside, that all is well, all is peaceful, and that abundance, including money, is always there and available to support the love and generosity of our fully open hearts.

26

THE MUTUAL SUPPORT GROUP

Since we are, in the most real sense, all connected, heart to heart and essence to essence, being in an environment that honors this truth is the most empowering environment for us. When a person is ready for consistent progress in her life, the most beneficial step she can take is to join a mutual support group.

The great value of the mutual support group is that it provides a setting in which participants are given the opportunity and encouragement to open their hearts and to feel their connection to the Oneness. From this place of open-heartedness and connection, giving and receiving love and support feels perfectly natural.

The power that comes from being mutually supportive can best be understood in terms of the principle of giving and receiving. This principle states that when a person gives with an open heart and with no strings attached, the primary beneficiary is the giver. This means that whenever any of us opens our heart and sends loving support to another, we have given ourself a gift. It also means that whenever we allow another to send open-hearted support to us, we have given that person a gift.

We cannot give from an empty cup. In order to give love and support to another, we have to be willing to open ourselves to receive the love that most of us have been resisting. There is no better place to practice opening to love, as well as sending out love, than a mutual support group.

When a support group is ongoing, it means that there is some degree of mutual trust among the participants. We trust another when we know, without a doubt, that the person will be supportive of us regardless of anything we say or do. Trust is feeling comfortable and safe in telling the truth to ourselves in the presence of another with confidence that what we reveal will not be used to hurt us.

While it may seem to many of us that we cannot trust others with truths that are very personal and sensitive to us, what is really going on is an inner conflict around the issue of trust that we are projecting outside of ourselves. The deepest part of us does trust that others love us unconditionally; however, the part of us that was taught to believe that others are untrustworthy does not. And therein lies the conflict.

The support group always expands whatever is going on within a participant. Therefore, whenever a participant is experiencing an inner conflict, the group will energize that conflict and make it more apparent. Remember, the conflict, whether it is a judgment about ourselves or another, or simply a limited view of a situation, is there to support us in opening our hearts to the feelings aroused by the conflict.

Feeling the energy contained in an inner conflict is the first part of the Feeling Exercise. One of the primary functions of the mutual support group is to provide a consistent and reliable environment of unconditional love and support for participants to go through the Feeling Exercise.

In addition to the Feeling Exercise, it is helpful for mutual support groups to incorporate within the format of their meetings one or more processes or exercises that can be performed by a person with an inner conflict with the loving support of the group. One such process is the Self-Empowerment Exercise, which is described in detail on page 189.

While one participant guides the person through the exercise, the other participants listen with unconditional love. There is no discussion and no advice given during the exercise, or for that matter, during the entire support group meeting.

It is the environment of unconditional love and support that builds the level of trust among participants in a support group. Each individual has the opportunity to expand his willingness to trust that his love for himself is strong enough to feel the feelings he has repressed in his judgment of another. He also learns to trust those who are supporting him, and to accept that their love and support is truly unconditional.

The more we trust ourselves and others, the more we allow our hearts to open and the more power we access. As we continue to deepen our level of trust, we come to the place where we are ready to surrender to others.

Surrender is just trust taken to a deep level. The ability to surrender to others is one of the greatest gifts we can give to them and to ourselves. A mutual support group in which the participants are in a state of surrender to each other is a group that creates great empowerment in its members. And each of the members takes that empowerment with her wherever she goes.

There is a hidden bonus of the mutual support group that, although generally overlooked, is nonetheless most significant and valuable. Since we are all connected, whenever anyone in the group opens her heart around an inner conflict, the rest of the participants receive the benefit of whatever expansion that person has generated. Furthermore, the willingness of the other participants in the group to join a person in feeling her feelings allows those participants to have the full benefit of the experience that the person has just processed.

Without a word of discussion, hearts are connected, experiences are shared, energy fields are opened, and unconditional love is expanded throughout the Universe. When we allow ourselves to be generous in the giving and receiving of love and support, we allow that generosity to extend to our experiences with money. We find that it is natural and fun to be generous to others and to ourselves.

Joining a mutual support group is the most direct route we can take to opening our hearts to ourselves and others. As we surrender to what is our natural environment, we access all of the loving support, nurturing and abundance that such an environment provides.

27

———◼———

A NEW VIEW
OF SURRENDER

When most of us hear the word *surrender,* we generally think in terms of a removal of defenses. We create defenses when we believe we are vulnerable and subject to attack. Our perception is that we are in danger, that someone can hurt us and that we must protect ourselves. This perception grew out of our early experiences with our parents and other key childhood figures who appeared to have power over us and who enforced their will on us.

As we begin to see the broader picture, we realize that we came into this life as volunteers who invited our parents and others to train us in their belief system. The overriding tenets of this belief system are that we are nothing more than physical bodies, that we are each separate from one another, and that we must compete with each other in order to survive.

Seeing and feeling ourselves as separate physical beings in competition with one another induces great fear in us. We then project this fear out into the physical world in the forms of murders, robberies, automobile accidents, diseases and so on. These and other reminders of our vulnerability are constantly in our faces, reported in detail in our newspapers and magazines, on our TVs and in films. They also appear in our places of business, in our schools, and as we walk down our streets.

What we are now coming to understand, however, is that we have created this seemingly overwhelming barrage of fear stimuli with great purposefulness—to bring all of our fears to the surface so that we are compelled to feel them.

For most of our lives, we have been trained to avoid our fears. We were taught that if we just ignored them, they would go away. Nothing could be further from the truth. Our fears not only won't go away; we don't want them to. For our fears are really wrappings around love.

Remember that there is only one energy in the Universe and it is love. We have immersed ourselves in a belief system that perceives fear as real and love as some abstract ideal. This system tries to make fear and love into opposites. In fact, they are two sides of the same coin.

However much fear we think we are feeling, we are really feeling that same amount of love. What we call emotions—anger, hatred, sadness, jealousy—are love distorted by beliefs.

When we are ready to feel our feelings fully and freely through an open heart, we come to the realization that all is love and that we are all One. This is the way we connect with our true power, which has always been with us but which we have tried desperately to prove has not.

The more intense our feelings, the more love and power there is to connect with. However, when the feelings are so intense that it seems as if we are unable to be with them alone, it is time to invite in the love and support of others. This brings us back to the mutual support group. It is through the support group that we are able to build enough trust in ourselves and others to begin to open our hearts and feel our connectedness. As our trust grows, our sense of vulnerability diminishes. It is then that we become willing to drop our defenses and allow ourselves to surrender to our Oneness.

When members of a support group reach this state of open-hearted surrender, they are in a position to provide each other with the most powerful support available, particularly at those times when it is most appreciated. For no matter how committed any of us is to this process of opening our hearts, there are times when our hearts do begin to close. As soon as we are aware of this closing, we can, in consciousness, feel our connection to the people in our support group and access power from them.

Feeling comfortable being in a state of surrender allows a person to access energy—power—from everyone. No matter what another person believes or how he is acting, he is always sending out energy. Each of us has the choice to open our hearts, feel our Oneness and receive the energy being sent as love, which is all that it is. We also feel this love as power.

With practice in surrendering, we learn to access power from every person and every circumstance. We then know that being in a state of open-hearted surrender is not only *not* a sign of weakness, it is the most powerful state we can choose to be in.

A few notes of clarification: Surrendering to another has nothing to do with approving of or agreeing with another's ideas or actions. It has solely to do with opening one's heart to another's heart, even though the other person may be attempting with great vigor to prove that he has no heart or that his heart is closed shut.

Nor does surrender mean resignation. Surrender is not a passive state of allowing things to play themselves out while we stay mired in a feeling of discomfort. To surrender is to consciously open our hearts and embrace in love whatever is in our presence or in our consciousness.

Surrender is a state of knowing that the power is within us, not outside of us. Whenever it appears to us that our power is elsewhere, we can reclaim our power by embracing it in our open-heart energy. The more we open our hearts, the more power we reclaim, and the balance of power in our relationship to the world around us shifts accordingly. We no longer see and feel ourselves as being at the effect of forces beyond our control. We realize that we are the source of power in the Universe and that whatever forces exist outside of us derive their power from our vesting it in them.

When we love ourselves enough to surrender totally, we realize not only that we are the source of our own power, but that we are always only in the presence of love—no matter how things appear outwardly. And we know that we can trust absolutely in our unconditionally loving Universe.

28

REACHING OUT
WITH COMPASSION

Because we are all connected, all part of the Oneness, whenever any-one is in discomfort, the rest of us feel the signals requesting support whether we are consciously aware of the request or not.

Our years of training in looking at the world through our physical eyes and responding from our intellects have taught us to shut out these requests for support through rationalizations. We can easily justify to ourselves and others why we can't possibly reach out in support of all the many people on our planet who seem to be in distress. Homelessness, starvation, political tyranny, child abuse, to name just a few, present overwhelming demands that seem far beyond our ability to influence in any positive way. So we turn our attention to those matters we believe we have at least some chance of influencing.

At the physical level, the many challenges we see all around us *are* overwhelming. As long as we see them as purely physical circumstances, they remain overwhelming and beyond solution.

What is most supportive to all of us is our willingness to broaden our vision—that is, to see beyond the physical. Physical challenges always derive from a breakdown in connectedness, a separation from the Oneness.

This is true both for the people who are having the challenge as well as for those who are observing it.

As an example, suppose I am reading the newspaper and I come upon an article about starvation in Somalia or some other Third World country. If I choose to respond from the narrow perspective of the physical, intellectual level, I see and feel the people of Somalia as separate and distant from me. I can either make believe that what they are experiencing is unrelated to me and turn the page, or I can feel a sense of powerlessness and resignation at the cruelty of forces beyond my control.

In either case, I have opted to close my heart and withhold love and support. Since we are, in fact, all One, I am not only withholding love and support from the people of Somalia, I am withholding love from myself and from everyone else on the planet as well.

Now I *can* choose to take direct action and donate my time or money to an organization that sends food and supplies to Somalia. This response comes out of a broader view and is certainly a more open-hearted and supportive response. However, it still deals with the situation at a purely physical level, and since the physical level is derivative—that is, a result rather than a cause—solving a problem at the physical level is not a true solution. The underlying dynamics that gave rise to the problem continue in full force and will perpetually recreate similar results.

This means that as soon as the problem of starvation is handled in Somalia, it will appear someplace else in the world. Our history books are full of examples of this truism.

When I am willing to broaden my vision beyond the physical, to open my heart and feel my connection to all other hearts, I reach the level of real power. In this state of empowerment, I feel the inspiration that brings with it true resolution.

It is important to remember that when my heart is open, I am sensitive to all the participants in the situation, including not only the people in Somalia who are starving, but also the government officials, the roving bands of outlaws and the warlords. My open heart does not judge the behavior of the various participants. Rather, the energy in my open heart connects with and stimulates the essence, the true power, of everyone involved. With continued stimulation, these participants feel the growth of their personal empowerment and the corresponding lessening of their need to seek power by manipulating others.

There are no bad people. There are many, however, who feel so powerless and victimized that, in desperation, they use whatever means they deem necessary to demonstrate how powerless and helpless they feel.

This brings us to what seems unfathomable to the intellect, the conscious mind. Because the true power in the Universe derives from the full and free flow of love, whenever anyone opens his heart and sends out love, deeply felt, that person is offering the most powerful support in the Universe. There is nothing that deeply felt, unconditional love cannot heal.

The big shift in focus that is required is from the physical to beyond the physical, from the conscious mind as the problem solver to the open heart as the true power vehicle. Once that shift is made, the rest is easy. Love works. It knows what to do, how to do it, and when to do it. We don't tell love what to do. We just turn it loose by opening our hearts.

One of the major challenges we face in our society and in many others throughout the world is the great disparity between the haves and have-nots, the rich and the poor. In our society, we have attempted to legislate solutions through social welfare laws and through tax advantages for creating housing and jobs in disadvantaged areas and for making charitable gifts to the poor.

Other societies have tried to lessen this disparity by using more extensive systems, such as socialism and communism. And individuals and groups within all societies have tried begging, pleading, marching in protest and even staging revolutions in an attempt to alleviate this disparity.

The extent to which these and similar methods have worked is not a function of the form that was used. It is a function of the degree to which the hearts of the participants were open. Open hearts expand into compassion. When we express our compassion, we are doing what is perfectly natural—not only generously sharing what is available but creating whatever else is needed from the limitless power of our inspired love.

When we feel compassion, we know the real value of money better than at any other time. We know that money is neutral and that it always supports us in the precise ways we allow it to. Our openness to the support of money and all other support is never greater than when our hearts are open and we are feeling compassion.

Our society, with its steadfast focus on money as part of a competitive-adversarial system, has encouraged us to overlook the great benefit of creating an environment of unconditional love and mutual support to resolve our challenges with money. My own experiences as well as those of hundreds of others have conclusively proven to me and to them that an open heart is not only helpful in resolving money challenges, it is most often the only way.

When we are able to feel compassion for someone who is making monetary demands on us or on whom we are making such demands, we open the way for harmonious resolutions that previously seemed impossible. The solution to what appear to be difficult or even hopeless situations is to send enough unconditional love with enough consistency that the recipient feels empowered. Remember, unconditional love, deeply felt, is the most powerful force in the Universe. When it is sent with great perseverance, unconditional love will do the job.

So life is about opening our hearts and keeping our communication channels open so that love, the only energy in the Universe, can flow fully, freely and steadily through us and to and from us. When our hearts and channels are open, the feeling of love just keeps expanding. This leads us to a state of peacefulness and inspires us to extend our growing feeling of compassion to others who have signaled their desire to receive this most powerful and empowering support.

29

THE SYSTEM
WE LIVE IN

Although our natural inclination is to be unconditionally loving and mutually supportive, this is not how most of us were trained to function in the world.

Ours is a competitive-adversarial system. Each one of us has been carefully taught since birth to integrate this system into our consciousness. We were never asked whether we liked it or not. We were just told that this is the way life works. And we have seen this system demonstrated all around us all of our lives.

The companion to this system is the hierarchical structure, which ranks each person according to how important and valuable he is deemed to be by the system. The incentive to compete is the rewards that are given—money, status, positions of authority—for making one's way up the hierarchical ladder.

Since money is the essential support for this system, those who are considered most important and valuable—top executives in major corporations, TV and film stars, professional athletes, high government officials—are rewarded with the greatest amounts of money.

If we take a close look at this ranking process, we'll see how refined it has become. Physicians stand higher on the ladder than chiropractors, who outrank midwives. CPAs rise above bookkeepers but aren't as valued as lawyers. With enough time and attention, we can create rankings with very subtle distinctions. This tells us how attached we are to this hierarchical structure.

In some instances, we need only look at a person's earnings to establish his position on the ladder, and thus his level of importance. Societal status and positions of authority are used to supplement money, although status and authority often bring to the holder access to money in indirect ways. An example is gifts from those who benefit from favorable dispensations made by people of status or authority.

This competitive-adversarial, hierarchical system is the one we entered into when we were born. Whether we accepted this system totally without question or rebelled against it, we have all been deeply indoctrinated in it. If those who rebelled think they didn't integrate the system just as deeply, the very fact of their rebellion proves that they did.

We do not rebel against what is not real for us. If I were to tell you that 2 + 2 = 5, you wouldn't bother defending what you know is true. Likewise, if someone truly knows that the Universe is an unconditionally loving and mutually supportive environment at all times and under all circumstances, he won't spend his time arguing the point. He will simply enjoy the benefits of what he knows to be true for him.

When we are honest with ourselves, we can appreciate just how much we have come to accept the competitive-adversarial approach to life. In fact, today in our society, most people believe that this system is the most desirable one in existence. This remains the consensus even though many people are suffering from the stresses of this system and the great anxiety that it generates.

How did this system evolve to become the mainstay of our society? It grew out of a series of assumptions, one of which is that people will only do their best when they have the incentive of competition. The implication here is that people perform with less than their full capability unless they are forced to by a system that only rewards them when they actively compete.

Another assumption of the competitive-adversarial system is that there is a limited amount of resources and that the fairest way to distribute these limited resources is through the competitive-adversarial approach. This belief is closely linked to the idea that society can afford to pay less attention to those who don't compete well in order to provide enough rewards to those who do.

Now let's take a look at this system in terms of Universal Principles, starting with the basic principle of our essential Oneness. This principle tells us that since we are each part of the Oneness, any attempt to disconnect anyone from the Oneness results in chaos and discomfort.

Whenever one person loses, we all lose. Whenever anyone is excluded, we all feel the pain of that exclusion. There are no exceptions. As we remind ourselves of our Oneness, we prepare the way for a system that includes and supports everyone—lovingly and equally.

Equality is not just a concept; it is the essential nature of the Wholeness. Each component in the Wholeness is the Whole, and we can only enjoy and appreciate the Wholeness when it includes everyone and everything. Therefore, until we are willing to open our hearts to everyone and everything, we do not feel the fullness of our joy.

Another principle that is useful to understand is the one that tells us that it is natural and fun for each of us to express ourselves by doing what we love to do. We don't need competition and the rewards of competition to motivate us to act in the world. We merely need to feel our connection to our Wholeness, which automatically connects us with our creativity.

And, of course, there is the principle of abundance, which has been covered repeatedly and underlies our broader understanding of the competitive-adversarial system. This principle reminds us that there are more than enough material assets, goods and services available for everyone. Thus, we have no need to compete with one another for these resources.

When we open our hearts to ourselves and others, we appreciate the ever-increasing value of each person who makes up the Wholeness. And we realize that each of us is far more valuable than any amount of money. As we become a society led by our open hearts, we will naturally create a system of mutual support and equality in which money flows freely, generously and in continuously expanding abundance.

30

THE ROLE
OF BUSINESS

We are a society that devotes a large portion of its time to business. It would be difficult to even consider our society continuing without business playing a dominant role.

With business as the centerpiece of our society and with so many people dependent upon their jobs in business for their livelihood, it is important that we gain clarity about the role of business in our lives.

Many of us define business simply as a vehicle to provide goods and services in exchange for money. We also see business as being separate from the rest of our lives.

What is helpful to understand is that our beliefs, attitudes and standards of behavior in business are the same as our beliefs, attitudes and standards of behavior generally. We may try to disconnect from our places of business when we leave them at the end of the day, but this is not possible. Our involvement in business is integral to who we are. This brings us, once again, to the concept of our essential Oneness. As we allow ourselves to feel our true connectedness, we recognize that business is just one of the many ways we express ourselves as we relate to one another.

Having defined business as a means of self-expression, the same self that is present in all other aspects of our lives, what are some of the ways that we can support ourselves in business? First of all, we can remember that the way we live our lives *is* our primary business. The narrower definition of business as the production of goods and services in exchange for money is just a small part of our larger business.

From this broader perspective, we can see that whatever factors enhance the quality of our lives in general are the same factors that will enhance the quality of our business lives. When we choose Universal Principles as the guidelines for our lives, these principles perfectly support us in every aspect of our businesses, whether we are in the role of executive, manager, employee, customer or investor.

Therefore, another way of supporting ourselves in business is to continually monitor our alignment or lack of alignment with Universal Principles. And since we are essentially feeling beings, the more deeply we connect with these principles at a feeling level, the more benefit we gain from them.

Among the major misperceptions in our more traditional view of business is that business is not a place for feelings or for an open heart. And it is certainly not considered a place to enjoy our sense of Oneness. Our willingness to move beyond these misperceptions allows our experiences in business to become the loving, supportive and creative opportunities they have the potential to be.

True creativity flows out of our open-hearted connection with our God presence. It is an expression that uplifts, benefits and supports *everyone*. Creativity is an expression of heart to heart and soul to soul. And it is inspired by that which connects us all.

We are each a perfect and essential part of a large tapestry that is continually expanding in size and beauty. Whenever any of us connects with his true creativity and expresses it, everyone feels the joy of this expression at her deepest level.

Our creativity is the source of our expanding abundance. The more we feel free to express from this loving part of ourselves, the more we add to the abundance on the planet and in the Universe. It is therefore to the benefit of each of us to support all others in connecting with and expressing their creativity.

How do we best support this free expression? By establishing environments of unconditional love and mutual support. In such settings, not only does creative expression expand, but all aspects of abundance expand as well. As we become willing to establish loving and supportive environments in our lives generally, we open the way to establish these environments in business.

As for money, it is helpful to continually remind ourselves that money follows, it does not lead. Whenever we try to move money into the lead position, we cause all kinds of havoc—in both our personal and our business lives. We have the world around us as a perfect example of what happens when money is placed in the lead position.

When our lives are aligned with principle, when our hearts are open and our God presence fills our being, money just naturally follows this alignment. And as the power from this open-hearted alignment expands, we eagerly and joyfully share the unlimited wealth that our infinite love produces.

31

THE TRANSITIONAL
PERIOD

A question people frequently ask me is: How does someone who recognizes the truth of Universal Principles, but has only experienced the competitive-adversarial system, make the shift into a mutual support system? In a large sense, answering that question is one of the purposes of this book. For a more concise answer at this time, we'll focus on what I call the transitional period.

The transitional period is the time when we are deepening our understanding of Universal Principles while we continue to experience the outplaying of our beliefs. It is a time when we are expanding our trust in what we know deep inside is true but which we haven't had the opportunity to experience as true on a consistent, day-to-day basis.

Perhaps most important, it is a time during which we are becoming willing to accept that everyone and everything is perfect just the way it is. There is nothing we have to do to improve ourselves or others or the world around us.

Accepting the principle of perfection, as well as all of the other principles, can be a challenge for many of us, because these principles run counter to almost everything we have been taught. It is a process that calls for taking small steps with patience and persistence.

The process generally begins at the intellectual level, since using our conscious minds is how most of us were trained to acquire information. During this stage, our minds begin to open and we expand our conscious awareness of how the Universe functions.

As we come to accept Universal Principles on an intellectual level, we move into stage two, where we begin to connect with them at a feeling level. This is unfamiliar territory for most of us, given that we have for so long suppressed our feelings. Feeling our feelings fully calls for a great deal of support and for continually expanding our level of trust in the truth of Universal Principles.

Let's take a moment to look more closely at this issue of trust. Where does our trust reside? It resides in our hearts. Our hearts are also the repository of our truth. We can only know what is true for us by opening our hearts to the truth and feeling how it feels. In addition, the more our hearts are open, the more truth we allow to come into our awareness and the more expanded our truth becomes.

As our trust in the truth of Universal Principles continues to expand, we become increasingly aware that every uncomfortable situation in our lives is showing us a belief we hold. This brings us to a seemingly contradictory situation. For as we open ourselves to accept the perfection of everything just the way it is, we come face to face with our beliefs, which make such acceptance seem impossible.

The solution would appear to be to change our beliefs. But as anyone who has tried this approach knows, changing beliefs doesn't work. We cannot change our beliefs for the same reason that we cannot change anything, be it a belief, a person or a situation.

We look to change something because we don't accept it the way it is.

In other words, we are judging the thing as bad or wrong. Whenever we judge anyone or anything, we lock the energy up tight around whatever we are judging and our relationship with the person or thing stays frozen in its present form. Thus, the result we achieve is precisely the opposite of what we set out to accomplish.

There is another reason why we cannot and really do not want to change a belief. Within each belief is the power that we vested in it. For example, when we believe in shortage, we give our power to that belief, and we will experience shortage continuously as long as the power remains there.

In truth, we cannot give away our power. But we can act as though we have and, more significantly, we can feel as though we have.

Whether our belief in shortage takes the form of poverty or endless debts or bankruptcy, the way to deal with the circumstances is always the same. We reclaim the power we have vested in our beliefs by connecting to all the feelings our beliefs arouse. We feel these feelings and the energy, the power, contained in them, and then we open our hearts to the feelings and to the power they hold.

In essence, then, the transitional period is a time of opening our hearts and reclaiming our power. As we invite in more love and more power, we not only increase our trust in what we know is true, we increase our trust in further opening our hearts and in allowing our open hearts to lead us.

32

ACKNOWLEDGING
HEROES

It takes a very powerful person to volunteer to enter a world in which virtually everyone is denying his true power. This power has never been lost. We have merely chosen to believe and thus to act as if we are powerless.

This sense of powerlessness is so pervasive that many people today firmly believe that they cannot take care of themselves. The old, the ill, the impoverished and the homeless are only the more dramatic examples of this belief system.

It is time to reclaim our power. It is time to remember that we are each so powerful that we can create any circumstance we wish. We are the sculptors, not the sculptures.

There is no way that one person can convince another of this truth. But when each of us is ready, we will know this truth, and this truth shall indeed set us free.

We are living in an age that encourages our readiness by providing increasing opportunities to glimpse our true power. And once the slightest reconnection with this power occurs, the desire to fully reconnect becomes an undeniable urge, an obsessive drive.

We are all heroes because we took on a heroic task. And whether we are still in the phase of making believe we are powerless or have begun the process of reconnecting with our true power, we deserve the acknowledgment that all heroes deserve.

As we silently acknowledge each other and feel gratitude for the courage we had to have to volunteer for such an enormous mission—to open hearts that have been closed for millennia—we can also remind ourselves that we are not alone. We have all been together on this journey and have been inspired to continue in support of one another because at our deepest level we know we are connected and we know we are the power.

It doesn't take the wings of a bird to soar past the clouds or the fins of a fish to dive to the depths of the sea. It takes the imagination and creativity of human beings to design and build the spacecraft and ocean vessels to propel us to uncharted frontiers.

We have the unlimited potential of a consciousness that is as expansive as the Universe itself. As we allow our vision to expand, we give ourselves more and greater opportunities to develop this potential.

What is it that inspires one person to have a vision that leads to creative expression while in another person the inspiration lies dormant? The answer is simply an open heart. Our open hearts are the source of inspiration and creativity as well as the source of joyfulness, harmony and abundance.

Our next frontier doesn't call for soaring the heavens or descending to the depths of the sea. Our next frontier calls for opening our hearts, expanding our vision and expressing our boundless creativity in loving support of each other. We begin, always, by accepting ourselves as perfect just the way we are, and then feeling so much love for ourselves that we realize that we *are* the joy, harmony and abundance we have been seeking.

The power and expansive nature of love is compelling our hearts to open and our vision to expand. As the process unfolds, we will find our-selves demonstrating the truth that abundance is the natural state of the Universe and that money is just one of the many vehicles we have to express the generosity of our open hearts.

From my open heart to yours, I hope that you have enjoyed reading this book and that you have gained at least a glimpse of the power of your open heart and the peace that comes from knowing that this power is always there for you.

APPENDIX

A SUMMARY OF UNIVERSAL PRINCIPLES

1. ALL ENERGY IS LOVE

Everything in the Universe is composed of energy, and this energy is love. All that we see and feel is an expression of love.

Because love is indivisible, we cannot love one thing or person more than another. Whenever we attempt to withhold love from anyone, we withhold love from everyone, including ourselves.

2. INFINITE INTELLIGENCE, OR GOD

Within love is contained Infinite Intelligence, which we sometimes refer to as God.

Love, Infinite Intelligence, God, is the source of all creative expression and the essential power in the Universe.

3. ONENESS

Since at the core or essence of everything is love, in the truest sense, *we are one*. When we feel our connection to our Oneness, we feel the power of who we really are.

4. PERFECTION

Our Oneness, God, is perfect and expresses this perfection in infinite ways. As human beings, we are created, and we function, perfectly just the way we are.

When someone or something appears to be less than perfect, we know our vision is narrow. Our vision expands as our hearts open. When our hearts are open wide, we see and feel the perfection of everything.

5. RELATIONSHIP WITH SOURCE

The way we view Infinite Intelligence, or God, is precisely the way we experience life. When we perceive God as a perfect and unconditionally loving and supportive energy at all times and under all circumstances, we experience true peace of mind and a life of total joy.

6. CAUSE AND EFFECT

Contrary to what we have been taught, we are not at the effect of the circumstances in our lives. We are the creators of these circumstances.

The knowing part of us, the part that is connected with Infinite Intelligence (often called the Inner Self or Higher Self), creates every circumstance in our lives. It does this so that we can feel the feelings these circumstances arouse. When we open our hearts to these feelings, we access our true power, which is the power of God, our Oneness.

7. FREE WILL

Infinite Intelligence accords each one of us the freedom to choose. We can choose for ourselves, but not for others.

We always have the choice in each moment to align our will with the Will of our Higher Intelligence. We also have the choice to adopt Universal Principles as the guidelines for our lives.

8. THE MIRROR PRINCIPLE

Everything that we see and feel is a reflection of the state of our own consciousness. This reflection is a gift, for it allows us to be aware of the beliefs we hold. We then have the choice to reclaim the power we have vested in our beliefs.

9. ALIGNMENT WITH PURPOSE

Everything and everyone in the Universe has a purpose for existing. We become aware of our purpose by opening our hearts and feeling our Oneness. When we allow the inspiration of our life's purpose to fill our being, we find that our lives unfold in inspired, fulfilling ways.

10. READING BODY SIGNALS

Our human bodies are magnificent instruments that tell us at all times just how aligned we are with our Oneness.

Discomfort in our bodies is a signal that we are withholding love. The greater the discomfort, the more we know we are resisting giving and receiving the natural flow of love.

As soon as we notice discomfort, we best support ourselves by focusing our awareness on our feelings, feeling them fully, and then feeling love for them and for ourselves. When we allow love to flow freely, our bodies reflect this free flow of energy.

11. EXPRESSING WHO WE REALLY ARE

Each of us has one or more talents we love to express. When we are fully and freely expressing who we really are, we feel joyful and supported.

If we notice discomfort in doing something, it is important to first come to peace with our feelings just as they are. The peaceful acceptance of one activity opens the energy to begin another.

12. GIVING AND RECEIVING

Giving and receiving generously is both natural and fun. A gift given out of true love and generosity—voluntarily and with no strings attached—creates joyfulness in both the giver and receiver.

13. ABUNDANCE

Abundance is the natural state of the Universe. It is the free flow of love, which is literally all around us and in infinite supply.

The more willing we are to give and receive love and support, the more open we are to those things that represent love and support. Also, the more gratitude we feel for all that we have, the more we open to receive.

14. MUTUAL SUPPORT

The Universe is a mutual support system. Every person and circumstance in our lives is there to support us by reflecting back to us the present state of our consciousness.

When we love ourselves, we attract the loving support of others. Meeting regularly with people who are willing to support one another in unconditional love is empowering to all.

As our ability to love and support each other unconditionally expands, so does our trust in the unconditional love and support of the Universe.

15. WHAT WE FOCUS ON EXPANDS

The more willing we are to see everyone and everything as a perfect expression of love, the more peace and joy we feel.

Our perceived need to focus on problems only attracts more of them to us. What we call problems are merely circumstances we created to put us in touch with our feelings. When we focus on our feelings rather than on the details of the circumstances, we connect to our true power and the source of our creativity.

16. NONJUDGMENT AND FORGIVENESS

Judging anyone or anything as being less than perfect blocks the flow of love. This creates discomfort within us that can only be relieved by opening our hearts, first to the judgment and then to the person or thing we have judged.

Opening our hearts allows forgiveness to expand into unconditional love.

17. MEANS AND ENDS

Means and ends are identical. The action and outcome are one.

We create peace by being peaceful. Inner harmony results in harmonious relationships. We experience abundance by generously sharing the abundance of our love.

18. LEADING WITH OUR HEARTS

Years of training have induced us to rely on our conscious minds to make decisions and plan our lives. But the conscious mind has neither the scope of knowledge nor the range of options available to it that our Higher Intelligence has.

Compulsively planning keeps us in our heads and out of our hearts. It is through our hearts and feelings that we access our Higher Intelligence, which is capable of guiding us perfectly at all times.

19. FEELINGS AND POWER

Our power resides in our feelings. The more willing we are to feel our feelings, the more able we are to connect with the power that resides in them.

The circumstances that we avoid are the ones that evoke the most intense feelings, and thus contain the most power.

The true power in the Universe is a totally peaceful power. It is the power of love fully, freely and joyfully felt.

THE SELF-EMPOWERMENT EXERCISE

When someone in a support group is feeling discomfort around a particular circumstance or situation, another group member can support the person by gently and lovingly guiding the person through the following eleven-step procedure. The other participants provide additional support by listening with unconditional love.

1. Describe the situation in as few words as you need.

2. Close your eyes and focus your awareness on how you are feeling. . . . Can you feel the feeling? Can you feel the energy, the vibration, in the feeling?

3. Are you willing to stay with the feeling and to allow it to be just the way it is?

4. Are you willing to receive support in feeling love for the feeling? Can you feel the support coming in?

5. Are you willing to accept the purposefulness of this situation, even if you don't understand what the purpose is at this time?

6. If there is someone else or others involved in the situation, can you accept that you attracted them to support you in reclaiming your power?

7. Take a moment and allow yourself to perceive the same situation differently. Let another interpretation come to you. . . . If you wish, you can share your insight.

8. Can you see and feel the perfection of what is just the way it is?

9. Go behind the apparent circumstances of the situation and feel the love in yourself and in all others involved in the situation.

10. Allow your heart to open and this feeling of love to expand. . . . When the love has expanded sufficiently, let it embrace the situation and all those involved in the situation, including yourself.

11. Feel love for yourself feeling all that love, and all the power contained in that love. . . . Feel that power as your own.

JOINING A MUTUAL SUPPORT GROUP

There is a growing network of mutual support groups that spans North America and Western Europe. If you have an interest in joining or forming such a group, write or call:

Celebration Publishing
Route 3, Box 365AA
Sylva, NC 28779
1-800-476-4785

The staff at Celebration Publishing will send you a list of people in or near your area who either are in a mutual support group or have attended an Arnold M. Patent workshop or seminar.

There is also available a Mutual Support Group handbook, which includes a summary of Universal Principles, a suggested format for a support group meeting, and various exercises that can be used during a meeting.

In addition to the two previous books written by Arnold M. Patent about Universal Principles:

You Can Have It All, Revised Edition (1991) and
Death, Taxes and Other Illusions (1989),

there are audiotape sets of weekend workshops and residential seminars led by Mr. Patent, as well as audiotapes of his talks on specific topics. To order the handbook, books or audiotapes; to receive a list of available materials; or to find out about upcoming workshops, call:

Celebration Publishing
1-800-476-4785